WOLF SPIDERS

SPIDERS DISCOVERY LIBRARY

Jason Cooper

Rourke

Publishing LLC
Vero Beach, Florida 32964

www.rourkepublishing.com

PHOTO CREDITS: Cover, title page, p. 4, 6, 7, 8, 10, 12, 14, 15, 17, 18 © James H. Carmichael; p. 19 © James H. Rowan; p. 21, 22 © Lynn M. Stone

Title page: *A wolf spider prowls the sand of its home—a Florida seashore.*

Editor: Frank Sloan

Cover and interior design by Nicola Stratford

Library of Congress Cataloging-in-Publication Data

Cooper, Jason, 1942-
  Wolf spiders / Jason Cooper.
    p. cm. -- (Spiders discovery)
  Includes bibliographical references (p.   ).
  ISBN 1-59515-450-7 (hardcover)
  1. Wolf spiders--Juvenile literature.   I. Title. II. Series: Cooper,
Jason, 1942-   . Spiders discovery.
  QL458.42.L9C66 2006
  595.4'4--dc22

2005010952

Printed in the USA

CG/CG

Table of Contents

Wolf Spiders

Wolf spiders are hairy hunters. And like their namesakes, they often spot **prey** and then chase it. But unlike wolves, wolf spiders hunt alone, not in packs.

Wolf spiders are a large group of spiders found throughout the world. Like all spiders, they are **arachnids**.

Like other spiders, wolf spiders hunt alone.

Some **species** of wolf spiders stay close to their burrow homes. Others wander.

Wolf spiders make silk, but they don't use silk webs to trap prey. Certain wolf spiders line their burrows with silk. They also wrap their eggs in silk.

The Carolina wolf spider is one of the wandering wolf spider species.

More than 200 species of wolf spiders live in North America.

Predator and Prey

Wolf spiders may hunt by day or night. Their night or day habits depend upon what kind of wolf spiders they are.

Hunting wolf spiders lie in wait for prey to come near. Wolf spiders have excellent vision. They are also sensitive to vibrations.

Excellent eyesight helped this wolf spider catch a grasshopper.

When a wolf spider either sees or senses prey, it hustles after it. Usually a wolf spider's prey is a small insect. But wolf spiders also tackle larger insects, such as crickets.

A wolf spider bites its prey with two pincer-like fangs. Big insects might escape the spider's fangs, but not its **venom**. Venom paralyzes or kills prey. While the venom does its deadly work, the wolf spider may use its walking legs and two mini-legs—the **pedipalps**—to grasp the prey.

Shown with its prey, this burrowing wolf spider lives in a silk-lined hole.

Wolf spiders are on the menus of larger **predators**, like certain birds, snakes, and frogs. Wolf spiders sometimes become the prey of certain wasps. The hunting wasp stings a wolf spider to paralyze it. The wasp leaves behind its young to feed on the dying spider.

The wolf spider's two spiky pedipalps reach out like tiny fingers below its mouthparts.

Where Wolf Spiders Live

Arachnologists have identified over 2,300 wolf spider species. About 230 species live in North America north of Mexico. Wolf spiders are among the most common spiders in North America.

One species or another can be found in

This wolf spider lives in the rain forests of Central America.

woodlands, meadows, swamps, deserts, grasslands, sand dunes, and rocky sea coasts. Many of the spiders that live on high mountains and in the Arctic are wolf spiders.

This night-hunting wolf spider lives in sandy soil.

A few
species live
in marshes
or at pond
edges. Most
kinds of wolf
spiders live
on the
ground. A
few species
are climbers.

What Wolf Spiders Look Like

Wolf spiders come in a wide variety of sizes. They range in length from just one-fifth of one inch (5 millimeters) up to just over 1 inch (2.5 centimeters) in length. Female wolf spiders are often bigger than males of the same kind.

The Carolina wolf spider is one of the largest North American wolf spiders.

Wolf spiders are successful predators partly because they blend in with their surroundings. They generally have earth colors, like brown leaves or bark.

Like all arachnids, wolf spiders have eight legs. They also have eight eyes, arranged in three rows. The eyes are at the front end of the **cephalothorax**. The cephalothorax is the first of a spider's two major body parts. The second part is the spider's **abdomen**.

Camouflage colors help wolf spiders hide and hunt.

The spider abdomen begins just behind the four pairs of legs, which are attached to the cephalothorax.

The Wolf Spider's Life Cycle

Female wolf spiders place their eggs in a silk **egg sac**. Many wandering wolf spiders attach the egg sac to their silk-making **spinnerets**. Burrowing wolf spiders keep the egg sac in their burrows.

Baby spiders, called spiderlings, look like tiny adults. Baby wolf spiders immediately hitch a ride on their mothers' backs. As they grow, they become large enough to live on their own.

Most wandering wolf spiders keep their egg sacs on their spinnerets.

Some female
wolf spiders
can probably
live three or
more years.
Males
probably live
just a year.

Wolf Spiders and People

A wolf spider can bite. The bite, however, is not dangerous.

Wolf spiders are more useful than most people realize. They kill many of the insects that people consider pests. Like all predators, wolf spiders help keep a natural balance of predators and prey.

Wolf spider babies ride on their mother's back.

Glossary

abdomen (AB duh mun) — the second major part of a spider's body the section that holds heart, lungs, silk glands, and other organs

arachnids (uh RAK nidz) — spiders and their kin; eight-legged animals with two major body parts

arachnologists (uh RAK nol uh jists) — scientists who study arachnids

cephalothorax (SEF uh luh THOR aks) — the body section of a spider that includes such organs as the eyes, brain, venom glands, and sucking stomach

egg sac (EGG SAK) — a case or container, usually ball-shaped, for eggs

pedipalps (PED uh PALPZ) — a pair of leg-like structures between a spider's jaws and first pair of legs

predators (PRED uh turz) — animals that hunt other animals for food

prey (PREY) — an animal that is hunted by another animal for food

species (SPEE sheez) — one kind of animal within a group of closely related animals, such as a *Carolina* wolf spider

spinnerets (SPIN uh RETZ) — finger-like organs on a spider's abdomen that release silk

venom (VEN um) — a poison produced by certain animals, largely to kill or injure prey

Index

Further Reading

Greenberg, Daniel. *Spiders*. Marshall Cavendish, 2001
McGinty, Alice B. *Wolf Spider*. Rosen Publishing, 2003

Websites To Visit

http://www.biokids.umich.edu/critters/information/Lycosidae.html
http://www.americanarachnology.org/

About The Author

Jason Cooper has written several children's books about a variety of topics for Rourke Publishing, including the recent series *Animals Growing Up* and *Fighting Forces*.